Since finishing our second book "LMNOP more creative lettering with Lindsay", there has b[een]
anticipation for the "XYZ" lettering book.

Let me just start out by saying that Lindsay Ostrom is an awesome lettering Diva. In my opinion she has gone way past her Queen status and is now a legend. I know of no one who has more imagination and willingness to share her talents with others. She gets such a thrill when someone comes up to her and shows them what they have learned from her books.

However, she is not the best speller in the world. So, having said that if you find spelling errors in this book do not be alarmed. She is an artist not an English teacher.

If you have bought ABC, LMNOP and now XYZ, and you have practiced, practiced, practiced you should be ready to graduate. Now there are no more excuses........ start writing............ and complete the certificate in the back of this book. If you see Lindsay and show her your lettering that you have learned from these three fabulous books, she will personally sign your certificate. Carry your book with you at all times. You never know where you might see her.

If you still can not letter like this, you can now buy the software! It includes lettering from all three books. Call Cut-It-Up for more information. This by no means, means we are finished with lettering books. We are just taking a small break. Oh by the way, if you like the cover of this book, next time you see Tom Breslin tell him he picked out great colors for the cover.

Miss Vicky "A.K.A."
"Ms. Every Thing" of Cut-It-Up
nickname by Bob...
of Scrapbook Garden,
Wichita, Kansas—♥

The ABC's of Creative
Lettering published by
EK Success/Zig.

LMNOP
and XYZ
Published
by Cut-It-Up

C000042289

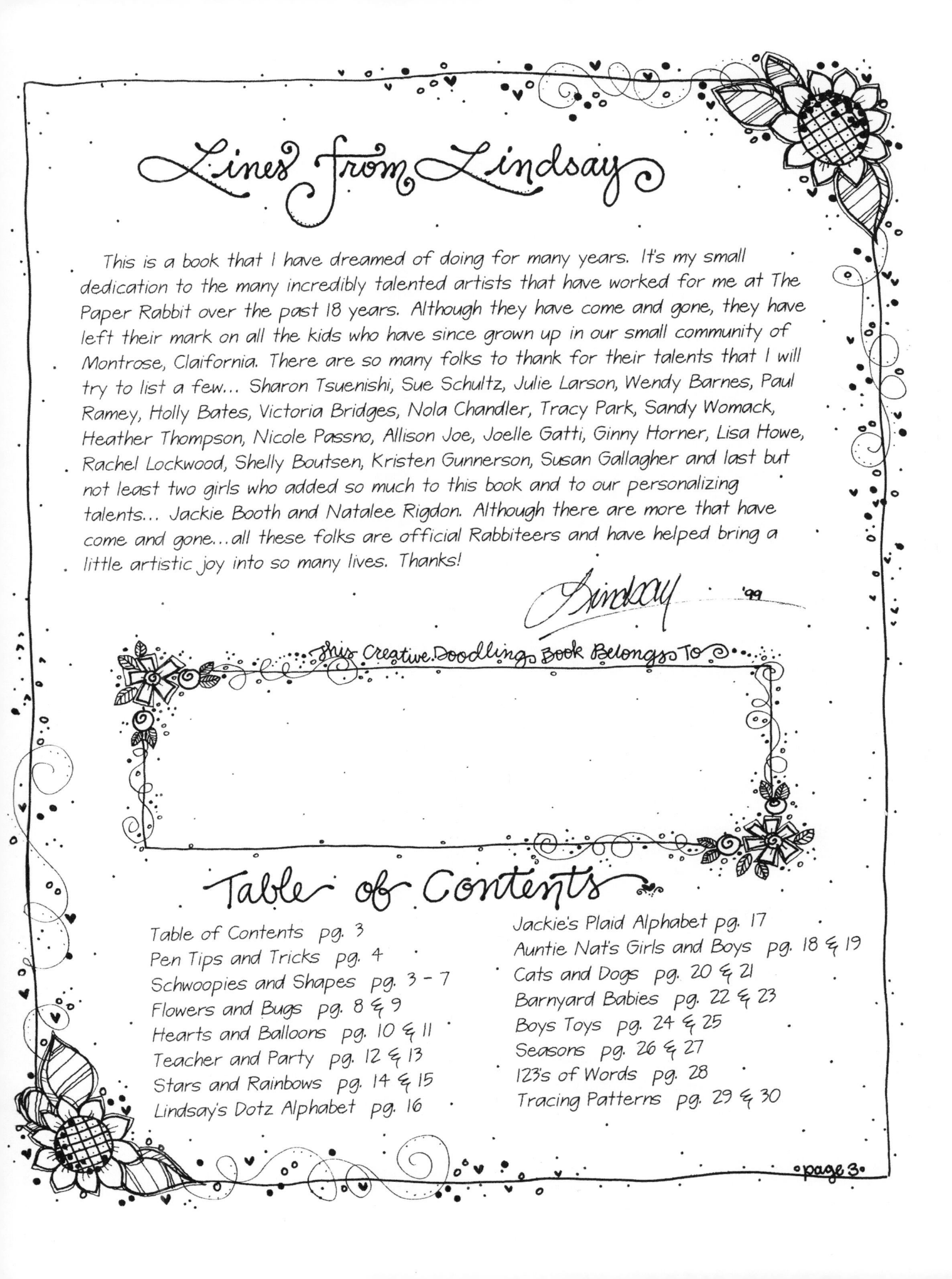

Lines from Lindsay

This is a book that I have dreamed of doing for many years. It's my small dedication to the many incredibly talented artists that have worked for me at The Paper Rabbit over the past 18 years. Although they have come and gone, they have left their mark on all the kids who have since grown up in our small community of Montrose, Claifornia. There are so many folks to thank for their talents that I will try to list a few... Sharon Tsuenishi, Sue Schultz, Julie Larson, Wendy Barnes, Paul Ramey, Holly Bates, Victoria Bridges, Nola Chandler, Tracy Park, Sandy Womack, Heather Thompson, Nicole Passno, Allison Joe, Joelle Gatti, Ginny Horner, Lisa Howe, Rachel Lockwood, Shelly Boutsen, Kristen Gunnerson, Susan Gallagher and last but not least two girls who added so much to this book and to our personalizing talents... Jackie Booth and Natalee Rigdon. Although there are more that have come and gone...all these folks are official Rabbiteers and have helped bring a little artistic joy into so many lives. Thanks!

Lindsay '99

This Creative Doodling Book Belongs To

Table of Contents

Pen Tips and Tricks

This book is set up to show you the basics of simple doodling. We have presented it in groups of shapes; starting out with circles and working up to squares, triangles and more. You can trace the shapes on pages 29 and 30 with our *Trace-it-up* acid free transfer paper on any item, you can learn the designs step by step with basic shapes. The designs can spruce up your scrapbook pages, greeting cards, letters and ok... even homework! But the designs will also work great on plastic and acrylic items like lunch boxes, clipboards, frames, storage bins and more. Whether you are working with paper or plastic, there are a few pen tips and tricks to use.

For scrapbooks and most paper items, there are a huge variety of pens on the market to choose from. Scrapbookers know that you need to choose a good acid free, pigment ink marker. To add to that I would suggest that you have several widths of these tips.. This way you can vary the size of your schwoopies, leaves and dots easily. Also try a little bit of ultra fine prisma glitter in some of your designs and lettering. Just a sprinkle using a clear liquid glue as the highlight in a balloon or for a snowflake can make a world of difference. Also try some of the great metallic markers out for balloon strings and streamers. You can also get some great effects with acid free colored pencils - these are great for shading. Mostly have lots of colors and tip styles to choose from; you can never have enough shades of green..... trust me!

For items other than paper you will need a paint pen marker. There are several brands on the market. Most work on all surfaces but some are specialized for ceramic and wood. These all have a shaking sound to them because there is a ball bearing in them. That's a good thing, you want to hear the ball rolling around. These pens are finicky and need alot of TLC so here's a few tips to get you going.

When you first unwrap the pen, depress the tip back inside the barrel quickly. This pops the bubble that separates the ink and oil and starts the mixing process. Put the cap on and shake it for a bit. Then depress the tip a LITTLE bit on a piece of scratch paper. The reason I say a little bit is because, in my opinion, once these pens flood and make a puddle on your paper, they never work well again! The starting process is a slow one. Keep repeating those steps (slowly) until you see the ink filling up the tip of the pen. Success! You can begin to write. Be careful not to push down on the tip or it will flood and create a big mess. Store the pens (and all pens) horizontally and if at all possible shake your pens for a minute or two every few weeks if you don't use them daily.

Doodling on plastic can be fun for kids and adults. It can also create heartbreak ! Let's say you flood the pen or mess up a piece... what can you do? We have found that nail polish remover, lighter fuel, acetone and some brands of adhesive remover will take off the paint. Test it first in a spot that you can't see. Some of those items will eat through certain plastic . Well... I think your ready to begin the doodling . Have fun and " Do It Cute" !!!!

Schwoopies & Shapes

The next few pages will take you through the basic daisy, leaves, vines or "schwoopie" and fill-in dots and doodles. Have fun!

STEP 1

the center of the flower always goes first and should

TIP*

always have as many shades of the same color as possible!

pink, pink
pink, pink, pink

STEP 2

the petal goes on next. Usually do 6 oval petals (or more) not round dot petals.

STEP 3

for more of a 60's flower power type flower- do only 5 petals and round them out. Also make the center larger.

STEP 4

add a shade darker, of the same color to any petal or leaf to make the original color pop out more.

STEP 5

Cluster them (and all designs) in groups of 3 - it's more pleasing to the eye.

STEP 6

if you've covering a large area, you can stagger them in a cemetrical pattern -2, then 1, then 2 or in a longer line depending on the finished size.

STEP 7

shaded leaf

veined leaf

schwoopie leaf

add some leaves. These can be ovals or have a pointed end. Cluster these near your daisy in groups of 3, 2 or 1 ... then vary them on each flower. Also add a shade darker to the leaf - as in step 4 of the daisy ... or try some tick marks for veins in the leaf.

STEP 6

add a schwoopie - start by making a string of "6's" - forward and backward and then relax the "6" string to have more flow.

ⓐ ← 1 "6"

← 1 upside down "6"

← another 6

ⓑ now try not to be too hung up on always making a "6".

ⓒ try to curl your ends & vary the width of the "6's" loops— small & large.

STEP 7

add schwoopies to flowers and then add some extra leaves, dots & smaller flowers (sometimes) to fill-in.

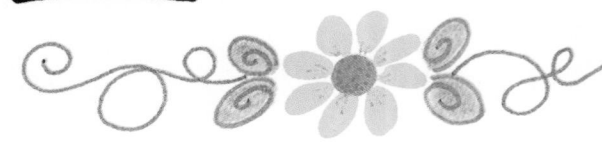

you can never have too many shades of GREEN when doing any flowers and schwoopies.

Dots can hide mistakes and add alot of flair. Try dots & many color combos and vary the size of your dots. Try "TRI-DOTS" to fit.

STEP 8

add some cool background fill & texture

Tri-Dots

variegated dots

Slashes

DOUBLE SLASH

Swirls

···· now lets put it all together ····

ⓐ and Voila ··· a daisy & schwoopie chain ⓐ

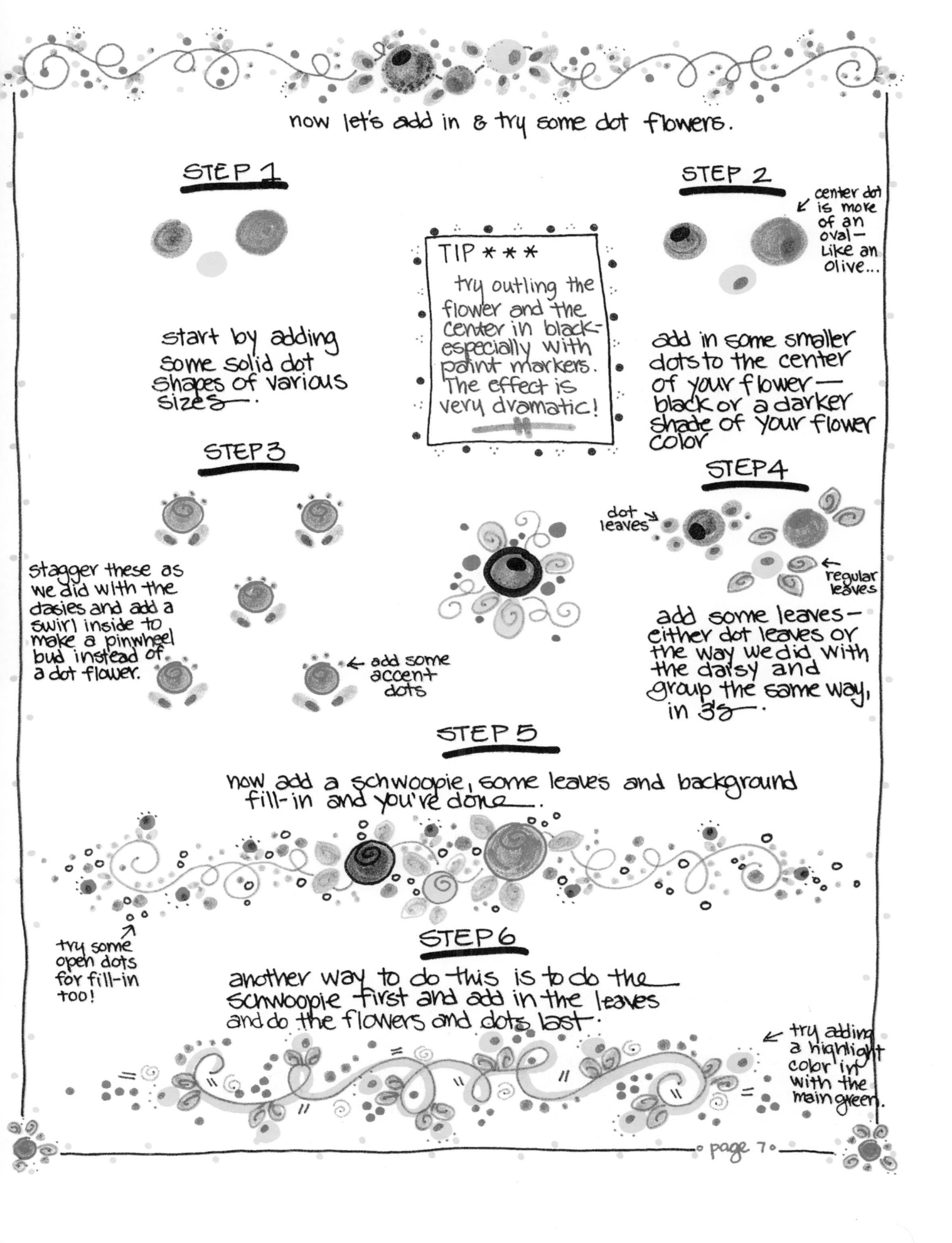

now let's add in & try some dot flowers.

STEP 1

start by adding some solid dot shapes of various sizes.

TIP * * *
try outling the flower and the center in black—especially with paint markers. The effect is very dramatic!

STEP 2

center dot is more of an oval— like an olive...

add in some smaller dots to the center of your flower— black or a darker shade of your flower color

STEP 3

stagger these as we did with the daisies and add a swirl inside to make a pinwheel bud instead of a dot flower.

← add some accent dots

STEP 4

dot leaves →

← regular leaves

add some leaves— either dot leaves or the way we did with the daisy and group the same way, in 3's.

STEP 5

now add a schwoopie, some leaves and background fill-in and you're done.

try some open dots for fill-in too!

STEP 6

another way to do this is to do the schwoopie first and add in the leaves and do the flowers and dots last.

← try adding a highlight color in with the main green.

STEP 7

← This outline shows how to outline the rosebud

try elongating the dot into more of a daisy petal and add a dot of darker color at the top - stagger these or do a vine.

STEP 8

now add a swirl into the dot of darker color & outline the bud in the same color. Add in some extra vines of a different shade of green and add some dots to fill.

Now let's add everything we've learned so far all together - a wildflower vine

try these other flowers to add to the wildflower vine

Vicky's Favorite Flower

this flower is done by putting 5 triangles together.

start with a small dot ____.

now add 5 triangles attached to the center dot.

← fill this in when done

try it larger by making the triangles more rectangular and start with a larger dot. Then embellish as shown above ____.

Lindsay's Sunflower

this flower is done like a daisy flower & pointed leaf petals.

start with a large center dot

now add small pointed leaf like petals- short & close to the center.

now add the detail - a grid in the center & some dots.

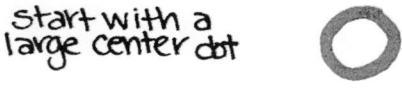

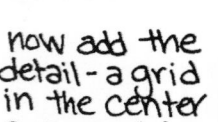

Try some ivy with your wildflower schwoopie...

STEP 1

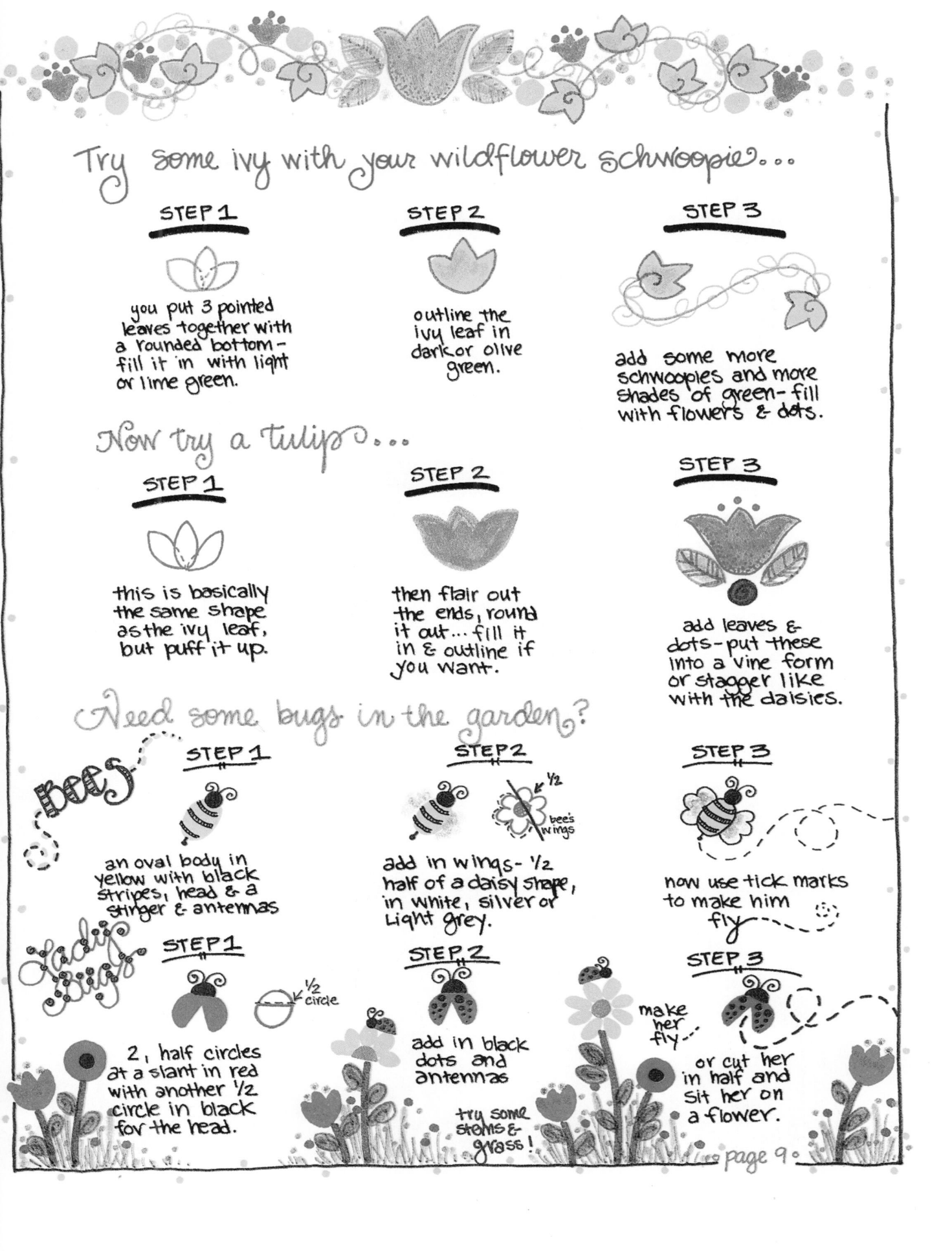

you put 3 pointed leaves together with a rounded bottom — fill it in with light or lime green.

STEP 2

outline the ivy leaf in dark or olive green.

STEP 3

add some more schwoopies and more shades of green — fill with flowers & dots.

Now try a tulip...

STEP 1

this is basically the same shape as the ivy leaf, but puff it up.

STEP 2

then flair out the ends, round it out... fill it in & outline if you want.

STEP 3

add leaves & dots — put these into a vine form or stagger like with the daisies.

Need some bugs in the garden?

Bees

STEP 1

an oval body in yellow with black stripes, head & a stinger & antennas

STEP 2

add in wings — ½ half of a daisy shape, in white, silver or light grey.

½ bee's wings

STEP 3

now use tick marks to make him fly

Lady Bugs

STEP 1

½ circle

2, half circles at a slant in red with another ½ circle in black for the head.

STEP 2

add in black dots and antennas

try some stems & grass!

STEP 3

make her fly...

or cut her in half and sit her on a flower.

The Cake Decorating Heart

depending on the marker you use... alot of hearts can be made by laying the tip of the marker down and pulling it (at an angle) down toward the right and another being pulled down to the left.

1st stroke → ↓ 2nd stroke

however the size of this heart can only be as large as the tip of your pen — these ♡'s are a good fill in design... quick n' easy!

So you still need to learn to shape a heart ...free hand! Don't Panic!!! Try tracing these. There is no rule for the perfect ♡...so choose the style that best suits you & your "look"!

Let's try some heart flowers ....

STEP 1

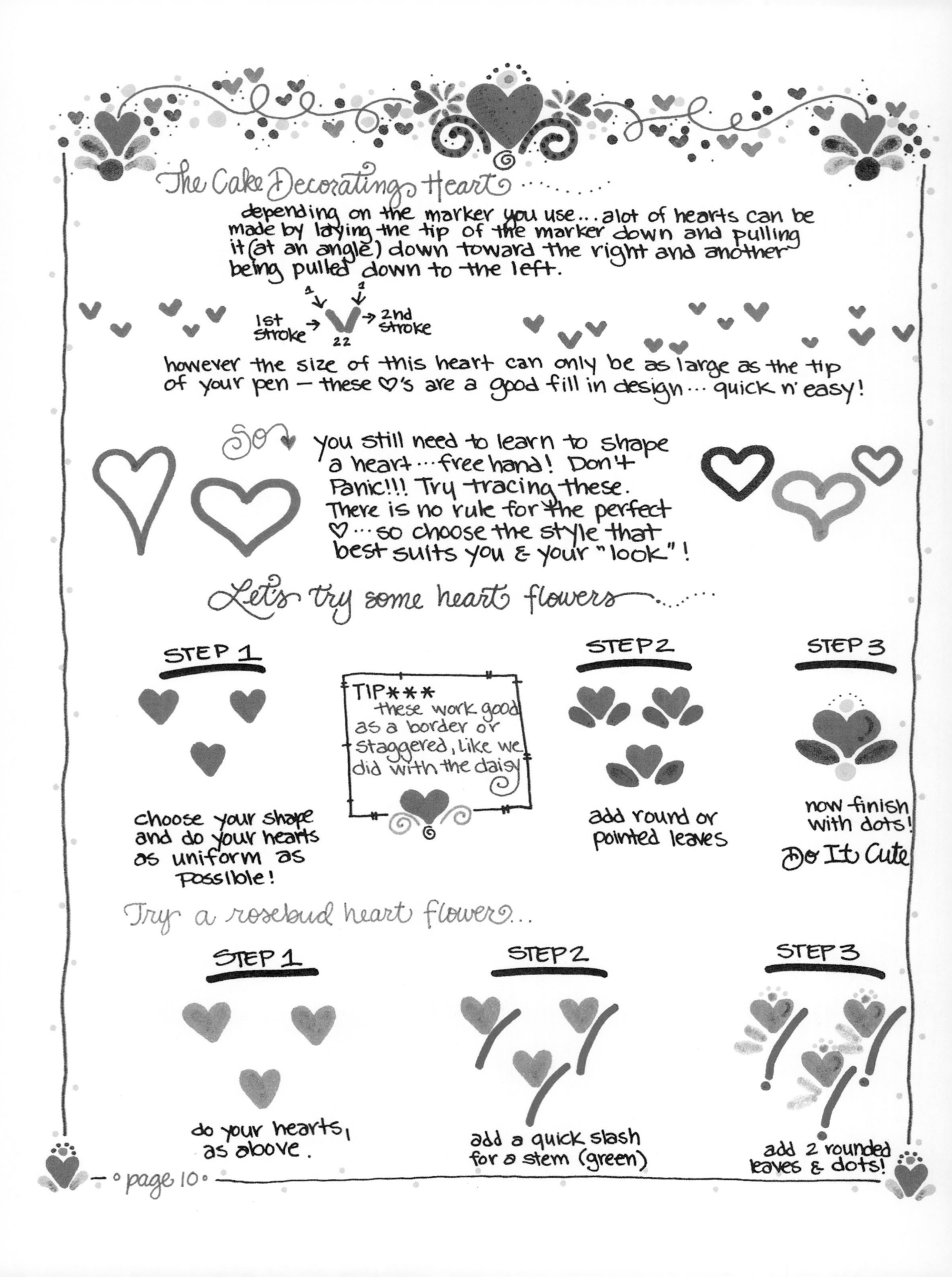

choose your shape and do your hearts as uniform as Possible!

TIP***
these work good as a border or staggered, like we did with the daisy

STEP 2

add round or pointed leaves

STEP 3

now finish with dots!
Do It Cute

Try a rosebud heart flower...

STEP 1

do your hearts, as above.

STEP 2

add a quick slash for a stem (green)

STEP 3

add 2 rounded leaves & dots!

Let's try a Scribble Heart

STEP 1

do a light outline of a heart — in pencil if possible, so you can erase. If not, do this in the same color as the scribble will be.

STEP 2

now fill it in with scribbles. Start at the top and go to the bottom right

STEP 3

now add some schwoopies and dots to fill — don't give up on this design, it takes practice.

How about a heart balloon

STEP 1

Start by grouping larger hearts in groups of 3's — fill them in solid.

STEP 2

now add a vertical schwoopie and 2 small rounded leaves at the base of the heart (same color as the heart)

STEP 3

add a highlight of white in the upper white corner and add some dots & hearts.

A heart butterfly?

STEP 1

smaller

larger

← bottom

make the bottom wing a bit bigger.

leave off the base of 2 hearts and lay them on their sides.

STEP 2

add a body, just an elongated oval, a round head & 2 antenna - all black.

STEP 3

add dots, outline and let her fly

And in keeping with our cropping off hearts theme........

Lets try an apple for the teacher..........

STEP 1

crop the base off of your heart (again), and do the outline in red.

STEP 2

now add a dimple or wave at the bottom & fill it in

STEP 3

try this in orange & it's a pumpkin!

add a stem— (an elongated triangle) and a pointed leaf & a white highlight line for shine____.

A crayon & a pencil are super simple.........

STEP 1

bring the tip in a bit.

draw a long, chunky rectangle and add a triangle without a bottom—to the____ tip.

STEP 2

for both, add a line for the eraser or the end of the crayon— and a jagged line for the pencil point or a straight line for the crayon paper.

STEP 3

add in the detail and you're ready to be an artist____.

GRAPES

← do this upside down, in blue and you have a bluebonnet!

a bunch of dots with a leaf & a stem & a little schwoople

C·H·E·R·R·I·E·S

yeap, you guessed it... just little hearts with rounded ends; a stem and some leaves.

Watermelon

hey a triangle →

a half a circle in red with 2 outlines in 2 shades of green with a few leaf-like seeds!

Let's Party with Streamers and confetti

STEP 1

make a schwoopie—but keep it very simple... not too many loops. We will thicken it up.

STEP 2

with a pencil or the same color pen—widen the line to make it look like ribbon—wind it in & out... thin and thick lines.

STEP 3

fill it in, and add a thin schwoopie in another color and then go onto step 4.

STEP 4

◎ confetti shapes... triangles, circles, moons, stars, hearts, squares & swirls ◎

now add a streamer...

.....and embellish

Try doing confetti a little larger for a cool geometric pattern

stagger this up & down to make a great border.

try a repeating pattern of colors... rainbow, pastel or brights

make it mod!

make the circle into a peace sign or ying-yang or add a flower power flower!

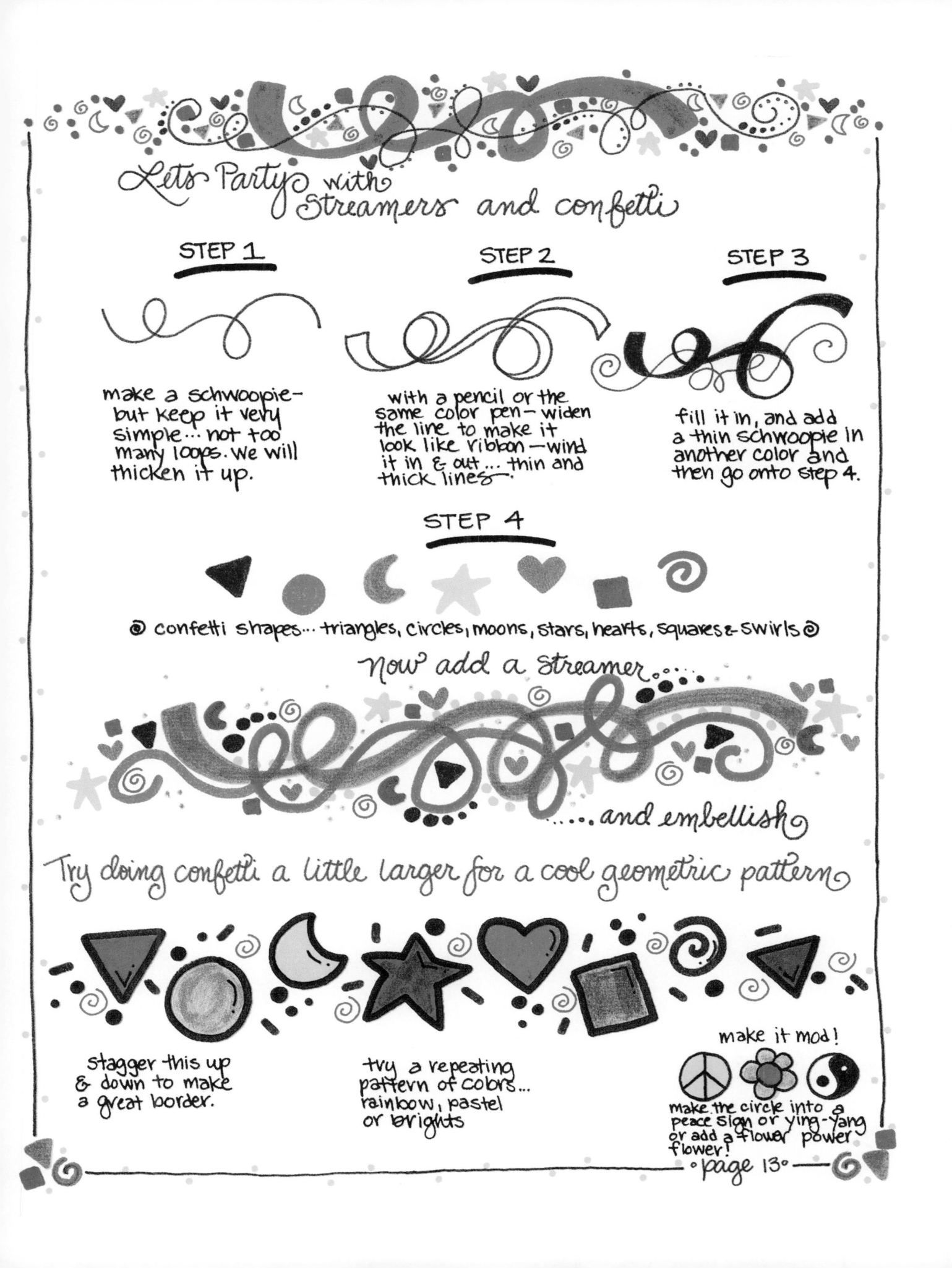

The Perfect Star . . . .
. . . . takes a little practice, start by tracing these shapes . . . .

. . . these are some basic shape ideas for open stars & starbursts .

now try these basic
5 pointed stars
and fill them in.

now make
a shooting
star . . . .

Try a Scribble Star . . . .

STEP 1

draw an outline
of a star - either
in pencil or very
lightly in the same
color as the scribbles
will be ____.

STEP 2

start scribbling
from the top left
point to the bottom
right point .

STEP 3

now add in some
5 pointed stars &
confetti and scatter
these or do them
in a border.

A Sunshine

This is just a circle; yellow or
orange with some lines
for the rays and some
dots for fill - use lots
of yellows & oranges.

QUICK
STARS

try some
simple
astericks
as
quick
stars.

A Moonshine

round
off

cut in
½

A crescent moon is
just a half circle with
2 curved triangles
added to the tips; now
puff it out a bit &
add a star or two—

Clouds & Rainbows

STEP 1

Forming a cloud takes practice. Do some scallops.

vary the size & shape. Now make an oval (in pencil) and placed the varied scallops around the oval.

STEP 2

now remove the oval, fluff up your scalloped cloud a bit and add some extra swirls & dots.

STEP 3

add in an arch of rainbow colors — with a single cloud or connect 2 clouds together & add some ♡'s for rain

Now let's take all the Schwoopies & Shapes we've learned & make a little personalized picture

do this for a gift on an acrylic clipboard, picture frame or box···· it'll be cute!

Riley

try some cute lettering and you are all done ————.

JACKIE'S PLAID

A B C D E
F G H I J
K L M N O
P Q R S T
U V W X Y
Z PARTY!

You Go Girls

By Natalee Rigdon

STEP 1   STEP 2   STEP 3   STEP 4   STEP 5

start with a basic circle and two tiny circles on each side.

make a "U" under the center circle. Make a triangle, then an arch at the bottom of the triangle.

add arms & legs & skin color to the neck.

the hair is a series of arched lines over & over.

Always do the face last to make sure the paint or pens are dry.

Now...
add detail to the girls. Using a fine black (permanent) pen to add collars, pockets, lace, dots, buttons and zippers.

Use... different shades of peaches, tans, browns for skin tones. Add accessories—bows, barretts, pony tails, braids & head bands to make their hair different.

Last... but not least change their faces a bit to give all the girls their own unique personalities.... you go girls!

I'm Tessa

Boy oh boy

By Auntie Natie

STEP 1

another simple circle, just like our girls.

STEP 2

make a "U" shape under the circle. The T-shirt & shorts are made up of rectangles, squares & triangles. Just refine the edges after you do the basic shapes.

STEP 3

add arms & legs and skin color to the neck.

STEP 4

hair is just ovals. start at the center-do it a little messy, it's a boy!

STEP 5

do the face last to make sure the pen is dry.

Now... add the detail to our little guys. Using a fine black (permanent) pen, add buttons, stripes, numbers, pockets, zippers and hats.

Don't... forget to use the peaches, tans & browns to vary skin colors and try lots of hairstyles & faces. After all... a boy's gotta look his best!

...I'm Connor...

53

Cats & Kittens

STEP 1

Start with the same circle as the kids face. (grey, tan, orange)

STEP 2

add 2 rounded triangles for the ears.

STEP 3

add 2 eyes, a heart for a nose, 2 swirls for the mouth and add 3 whiskers.

STEP 4

now add her body - an oval shape with 2 scalloped feet. Repet for back.

STEP 2

add in her tail & feet/leg detail (fill-in). And outline with a darker color.

STEP 6

add details - stripes and an outline

STEP 1

kind of a jellybean shape for the body with extra scallops for the feet. Add a circle for the head.

STEP 2

Add ears (as above) and a thin jellybean tail. Outline in a darker color.

STEP 3

add scribble stripes whiskers and she's done.

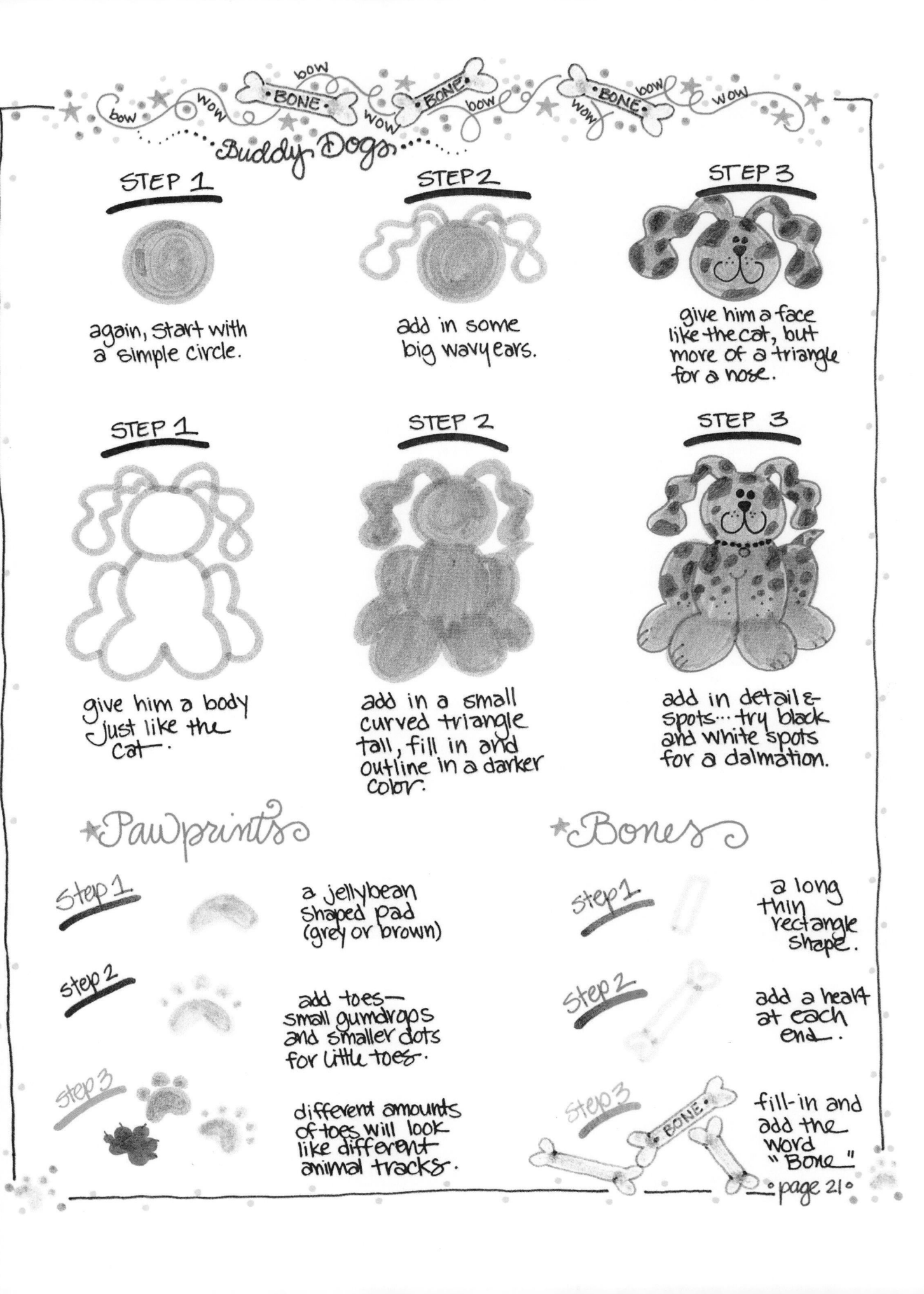

Buddy Dogs

STEP 1
again, start with a simple circle.

STEP 2
add in some big wavy ears.

STEP 3
give him a face like the cat, but more of a triangle for a nose.

STEP 1
give him a body just like the cat.

STEP 2
add in a small curved triangle tail, fill in and outline in a darker color.

STEP 3
add in detail & spots....try black and white spots for a dalmation.

Pawprints

Step 1 — a jellybean shaped pad (grey or brown)

step 2 — add toes— small gumdrops and smaller dots for little toes.

Step 3 — different amounts of toes will look like different animal tracks.

Bones

step 1 — a long thin rectangle shape.

step 2 — add a heart at each end.

step 3 — fill-in and add the word "BONE"

Barnyard Babies

~ BUNNIES ~

STEP 1

make a jellybean shaped body and add a circle for the head.

STEP 2

now make 2 large ears by forming a full heart shape & a round tail.

STEP 3

add pink to the center of the ears — fill-in & add a round nose, eyes & whiskers.

~ SHEEP ~

STEP 1

the same way we did the cloud, works for sheep. Make an oval and add scallops around it.

STEP 2

← ears

↑ nose

Now give her a head (oval shaped), 2 ears (heart shaped), feet (4 rectangles) & a little tail.

STEP 3

fill it all in.... and you can almost hear her go Baa !!!

~ PIGGIES ~

STEP 1

↓ snout shape

Start with an oval and add a small square to the snout area.

STEP 2

→ feet are a combo of rectangles & triangles

add a ♡ for ears, 4 rectangle feet & schwoople tail.

STEP 3

← tail

add darker pink accents & blk. eyes!

DUCKS

STEP 1

half a circle

a half circle with a dip in the center for the body.

STEP 2

add a circle for the head and give a little curl to the tail.

STEP 3

add a beak by forming 2 little leaf shapes in orange. Add stick figure type feet and make your duck walk.

TEDDY BEAR

STEP 1

ear shape from a circle

do a simple circle for the head and 2 ½ circles for the ears.

STEP 2

make an oval shape to form his body.

STEP 3

add feet & arms by attaching a ½ square to the body and add circles to that for the paws.

STEP 4

now give him some cute detail and outline him.

Try doing him in black & white to make a cute Panda

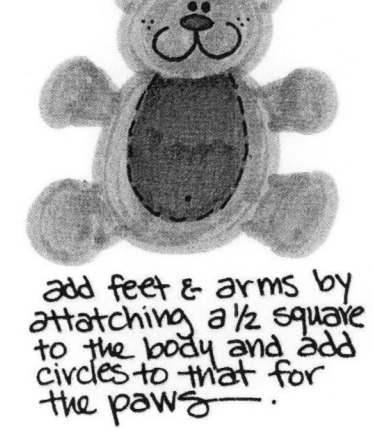

Boys Toys

= Trains =

• Caboose •
STEP 1

• Cars •
STEP 2

• Engine •
STEP 3

The train is done as a series of squares & circles shapes. Each piece, shown above, just gets filled in.... outlined and given some detail. Finish with a track of checks and some smoke. Try this by doing each car at an angle - staggered, to show movement.

= Boats =

STEP 1

the boat is a rectangle with angled ends.

STEP 2

add a line for a mast an 2 triangles for the sails.

STEP 3

add a little flag at the top and some detail and you're ready to sail.

= Balls =

Baseball

~ stitches are just v's.

a white circle with block lines & red stitching.

Basketball

just an orange circle with brown lines for detail.

Football

GO VIKINGS

a pointed oval shape with black & white detail lines.

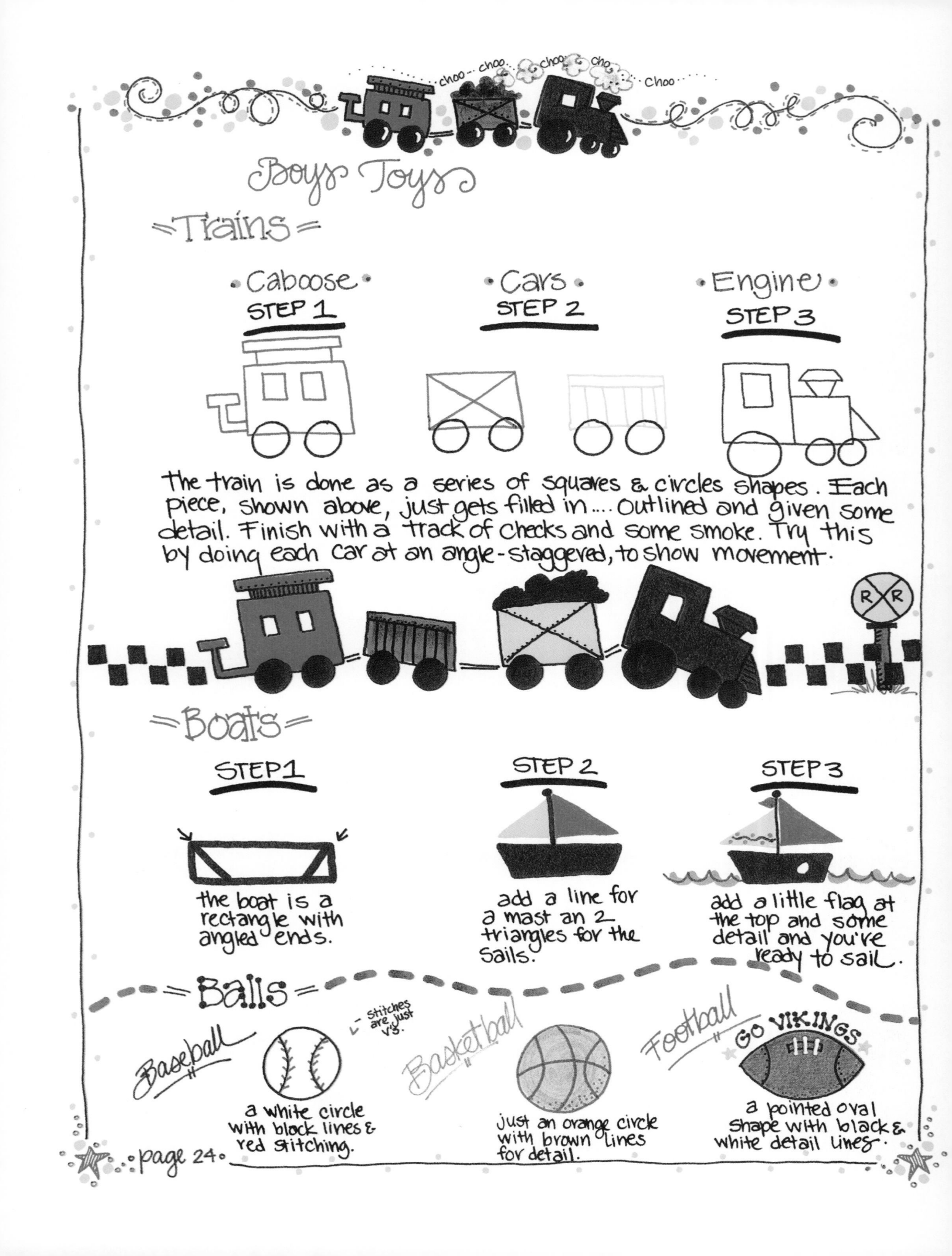

= Car =

STEP 1

There is no easy way to explain now to draw the car body in shapes. The best way is just to trace it until you feel comfortable to do it on your own.

STEP 2

add in wheels and a convertable top (long leaf shapes), a windsheild and a steering wheel.

STEP 3

add some bumpers & detail - don't forget the antenna for the tunes and a road to drive on.

= Plane =

STEP 1

the basic body is a rounded rectangle that gets narrower at the tail.

STEP 2

add some wings, just rectangles and leaf shapes for the tail. Leave space for detail stripes.

STEP 3

fill it in and add your detail lines and colors.

STEP 4

add in any last details, some puffy clouds, some dash marks to show flight and let her soar.........

= Balls =

Soccer

a round white circle with black detail - just triangles and squares.

Tennis

green or yellow circles with detail lines, same as the baseball.

Volleyball

start here!

a white circle with black lines. start with a Y

page 25.

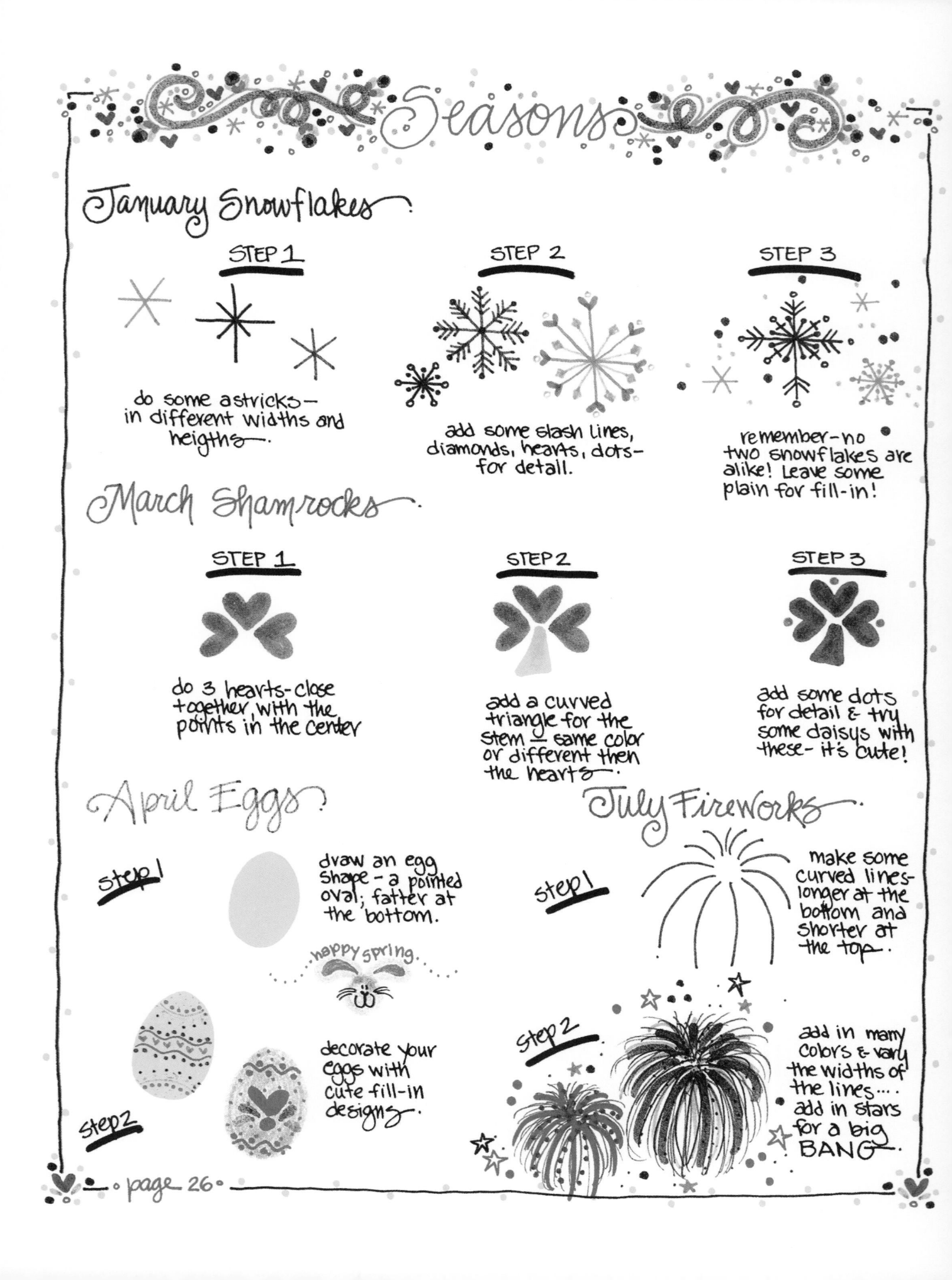

Seasons

January Snowflakes

STEP 1
do some astricks— in different widths and heigths.

STEP 2
add some slash lines, diamonds, hearts, dots— for detail.

STEP 3
remember—no two snowflakes are alike! Leave some plain for fill-in!

March Shamrocks

STEP 1
do 3 hearts-close together, with the points in the center

STEP 2
add a curved triangle for the stem — same color or different then the hearts.

STEP 3
add some dots for detail & try some daisys with these- it's cute!

April Eggs

step 1
draw an egg shape - a pointed oval; fatter at the bottom.

happy spring.

step 2
decorate your eggs with cute fill-in designs.

July Fireworks

step 1
make some curved lines- longer at the bottom and shorter at the top.

step 2
add in many colors & vary the widths of the lines.... add in stars for a big BANG.

October Pumpkins

STEP 1

draw a basic apple shape (pg.12)— but a bit larger.

STEP 2

add a stem, a leaf and a little schwoopie vine.

STEP 3

add a face for a jack-o-lantern - just triangles and squares and lines for detail.

November Acorns & Leaves

STEP 1

the top is a half of a circle with a small stem and the bottom ½ an oval with a small point.

STEP 2

the leaf is a Miro shaped leaf with wavy scallops and a stem .

STEP 3

do these scattered or as a border with some random shapes in between- try a schwoopie in gold.
(Thanks Tamara for this design!)

December Holly

Step 1

the leaf is a scalloped shape- but the scallops face the inside of the leaf - the points face out.

Step 2

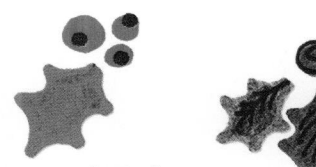

add some berries - group holly & berries in 3's or alone. Add dots to the berries and veins to the leaves ~ try gold veins.

December Pinebough

step 1

do a very simple schwoopie

step 2

add slash lines at an angle for the pine needles.

step 3

add some berries & dots - this works great in corners or borders.

Try adding some of the doodles and designs that you have learned to some words for personalizing your pictures.

daisies and schwoopies

MOM

SPRING

tulips & ladybugs

balloons & confetti

HAPPY BIRTHDAY

#1 Teacher

apples and pencils

Little girls

bunnies and ducks

BABY

Tessa

IT'S A BOY

sports balls

Happy Holidays

holly and berries schwoopies and dots!

Use these black and white line drawings with a light box or our "Trace-it-Up" acid-free tracing paper to trace these designs onto plastic, glassware, ceramic and more. Enlarge or reduce these designs on a copy machine first.

daisy

schwoopie

dot flower

sunflower

rosebud

vicky's flower

tulip

bumblebee bee

ladybug

apple

pencil

crayon

streamer

confetti shapes

star

heart

happy sun

cloud

rainbow

Girl

Boy

grass & flowers

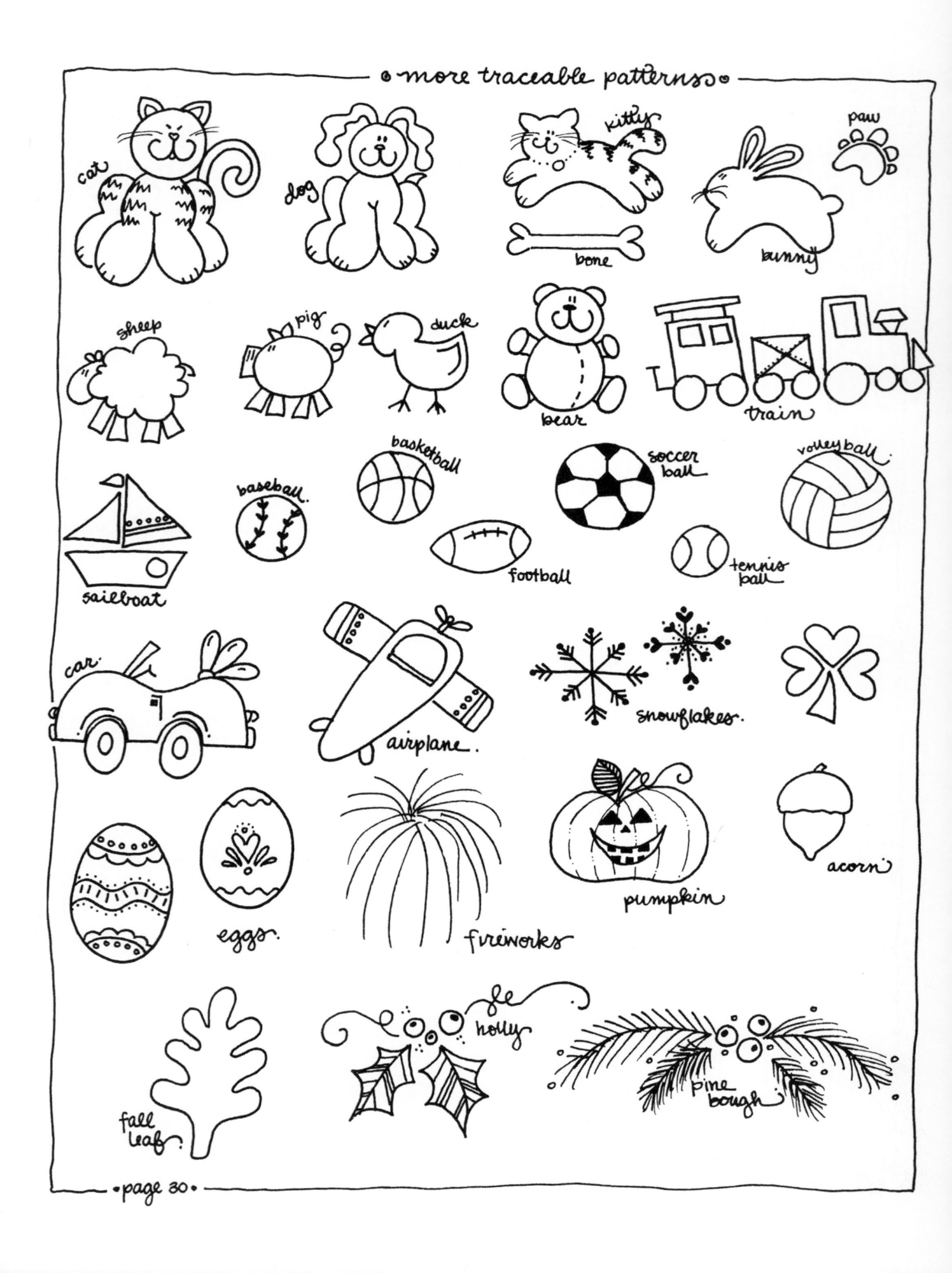

cat

dog

kitty

paw

bone

bunny

sheep

pig

duck

bear

train

baseball

basketball

soccer ball

volleyball

sailboat

football

tennis ball

car

airplane

snowflakes

eggs

fireworks

pumpkin

acorn

fall leaf

holly

pine bough

Now I know my ABC's lettering guide

• to be used with LMNOP more creative lettering by Lindsay •

45° angle
← angle
line your pen tip here!

45°
angle

turn
your book/
flip here!

Now I Know my ABCs lettering guide ©

· to be used with I KNOW more creative lettering by Lindsey) ·

Printed in Great Britain
by Amazon